.... a shameless

desolate,

hungry present.

a poem by

Alf E.F. Muronda

ISBN   978-1-965398-07-4
© Elfigio F Muronda   Published 2025
Publisher: MASAKA PUBLISHING MEDIA HOUSE
alf@cp7sisters.com

For our family heroes who gave it all so we could be –
Richard Lawrence Tichatonga Muronda
Denis "Chigondi" Nyagwaya
Big Boy Chirikumarara.

Thank you

…a shameless, desolate, hungry present

He looked around him,

the deflected sunlight in the cave

reflected a dim luminescence on the rock walls of

the cave.

The air was cool and dry.

      Fifteen weary men lay sprawled on the dirt floor.

      each lost in his own fantasy of what food and

      clean water tasted like.

Each fighting his own war with his own stomach.

Their eyes may have been closed

      but a man can only sleep so much.

Their armour stood silent guard against the rock

walls staring with pity at these desperate

      would-be masters.

      He crawled to the mouth of the cave.

He thought he had felt a twinge in his bowels

       to relieve himself.

No one paid him any attention.

He was a leader with nothing to give,

       a ghost that had used up all its heavenly favors.

They knew he was as hungry as they were

       and surely

       if he had the power of Chaminuka.

He would have turned stone into bread by now.

He was just a man,

       there was no point in taunting him with the fact.

He stuck his head out of the cave.

The laser sharp rays of the hot afternoon sun

       hit his eyes.

He searched for the man on sentry duty.

He saw him.

He was sitting fifty yards away under a tree
        that had lost its dignity as a tree
        when it lost its conception
            of what a tree is supposed to be.

It was leafless.
Its limbs stood out like bundled turfs of hair
        on the head of a demented person.

He waved at the sentry.

The sentry waved back with the slightest
        movement of a finger.
The hot dry sun had sapped all his energy.
He wondered over to the huge dead msasa tree
        on the other side.

He stood under the tree.

The guerrilla warfare trained animal instinct in him
scanned

> the rock outcrops around the dead tree and

> the desert like terrain in its perimeter

> and beyond.

His hand casually caressed

> the butt of the ak47 assault rifle on his shoulder.

His mind absorbed the topography of the area

> comparing what he saw

> with something already stored in his mind.

everything was still…

No man dared the insufferable heat.

The beasts of the forests had long gone.

> and the flies had fled underground.

A large solitary lizard was the exception.

It sunbathed itself, on what,

        he vividly imagined

        was a hot burning rock.

It seemed suspended between

        the oppressive scorching rays of the sun and

        the baking hot reflective surface of the rock.

        Had it not been for the regular respiratory

        movement under its thorax

        he would have presumed it dead.

He turned his eyes to the sky shielding them

        with his open hand…

    From far away

    I heard the anguished cry of a newborn.

    it was the cry of Afrika's man-child on its first

instance on earth.

I shook my head in sorrow,

      because it was too late then.

His umbilical cord had been severed and buried.

I shouted into the wind and admonished

      "You cannot go back into your mother's womb.

You are on your own,

son of the soil…"

Hither and thither
      bleached dry broken animal bones
      lay forlorn on the cracked hard earth
      bearing miserable testimony
      to the life that had once encased them.

The rivers that had run with vivacious fury

       through the valleys

       had turned into gaping gullies

       broad meandering sandy furrows

       that looked

       ugly and purposeless.

His fingers fumbled over the pockets of his dirty shirt

       and found a pinch of dry coarse tobacco

       and a piece of an old newspaper.

Mechanically,

       He began to roll himself a cigarette.

       He patted his pockets for matches.

       He went through his fatigues

           pocket by pocket.

       He did not find the accursed matches.

       His evil filled eyes stared at the crudely rolled
cigarette and cursed it silently

           throwing it away.

Slowly, he lowered himself down

and slumped under the tree.

His scuffed boots

dug into the hard dry soil for support.

He searched hopelessly in the sky

for a cloud

even a speck of a cloud.

His faltering belief argued with his sanity

surely there used to be a life giving

topical rain from that same sky.

Or was his mind deranged?

For the sake of his sanity

his eyes searched again,

searched for anything,

any kind of sign to reassure him

that he had not been transported

unconsciously

      by some conjuration of the white man

      or by some quirk of evil fate

      been transported to another time

      another place

      another country

      a desolate, god forsaken, barren no man's land.

He needed a reaffirmation

      that this was still the same country

      that his ancestors had bequeathed him.

      That this was the same country

      they had shed their blood in

      to fertilize its soil for his seed.

His heart longed for the spittle

      from a mother's lips to her sickly child.

Will you mother-cursed sky, please tell me.

      Is this the same country

that we have become orphans for,

fair game to the guns of war

and the incisor of the nocturnal hyena?

Is this the land of our forefathers' graves

or is it

a treacherous harlot of the yellow bearded

white man?

Have the spirits of our ancestors lost

yet another battle to the white man's foreign

gods?

Answer me!

Do you hear me, you mother fornicating sky?

There was no answer.

His remonstrations went the way of the wind.

He was met by the stare of an ungodly, vacant

celestial dome.

It had no interest in him

just as it had no interest in the patched earth

he was standing upon.

In all directions

the empty sky stretched into the horizons

dragging sheets

upon shimmering sheets of heat waves

that scotched the brown earth in their wake.

The world had become a shadowless wasteland

the grass had died and withered

into chaff in the wind.

Bark stripped trees stood

like shameless dismembered human figures, dead

and improperly interned in grotesque upright

caskets.

He tried to think

but no thought had enough power to firmly

grip his mind.

A myriad curses found favor with his tongue.

Curses upon the sun

for its heartlessness, and curses upon the earth

for its cowardly surrender.

However, he soon ran out of strength,

     his extortion, the curses, and threats on the

     sun and earth went the way of the wind.

He just sat there, indolent.

Even the prime mover,

     the thought that he had wanted to relieve himself

     the thought which had brought him here

     to the huge dead msasa tree

     to relieve himself

     was now too weak to push him into the action.

Like the man on sentry duty

     he sat under the tree that had lost

     its conception of what a shade was supposed to
be.

His hands groped the ground aimlessly.

They found a twig and broke it in two.

and threw it away.

His tortured soul and his troubled mind

irritated his body.

Seasoned by the years of the hard war he lived,
       his body froze
       and
       ignored the heat of the sun
       and the rough pressure of the dry bark
       of the dead tree on his back.

Like the lizard on the hot baking rock,
       he was suspended against the tree.

With each measured breath,
       the warm air circulated through
       his broad African nose and
       into his blood like an opiate.

Time went by in no particular sequence.
       It had no direction either.

Time and his mind had wed,
       their wedding bed was now hovering above
       in the dry empty sky
       knowing not
       whether to leap into some glorious
       illusionary future

or to return to the familiar hounds of yesterday

through the valleys of often re-lived triumphs

and gullies of painful

but time cured memories.

The present,

       this wretched offspring of an apathetic god,

       this indubitable testament

       of human impotence

       in the face of a deaf and hostile natural force,

       he banished away.

       Locked it in its own infernal ignominy

       as another familiar past

       endured and conquered,

       until

       it too

       was suspended.

The wonderous union of time and his mind

       eloped to his yesterdays

       his childhood

       his political puberty

       and maturity.

In the crevices of his yesterdays
    he hoped
    the union would find and bring to the present
    some semblance of logic
    some purchase
    that could possibly justify

this shameless, desolate, hungry present.